I0439666

Fair Lending Analysis of Mortgage Pricing:

Does Underwriting Matter?

Yan Zhang

Office of the Comptroller of the Currency

OCC Economics Working Paper 2010-1

Keywords: Mortgage lending, underwriting, pricing, fair lending analysis, differential treatment, sample selection bias, omitted variables
JEL Classifications: C34, G21, J78, R20

The views expressed in this paper are those of the author and do not necessarily reflect the views of the Office of the Comptroller of the Currency or the U.S. Department of the Treasury. The author would like to thank Jason Dietrich, Irene Fang, Gary Whalen, Irina Paley, and Lily Chin for their insightful comments and editorial assistance.

Please address correspondence to Yan Zhang, Senior Financial Economist, Compliance Risk Analysis Division, Office of the Comptroller of the Currency, 250 E Street, S.W., Washington, DC 20219 (phone: 202-874-4788; e-mail: yan.zhang@occ.treas.gov).

Fair Lending Analysis of Mortgage Pricing: Does Underwriting Matter?

Yan Zhang

Office of the Comptroller of the Currency

Abstract: This paper focuses on potential interaction between the mortgage underwriting and pricing decisions for fair lending analysis of mortgage pricing. We argue that the loan approval or denial decision determines the loan origination population and therefore the underwriting policies might affect the fair lending assessment of the subsequent pricing decisions. The paper also finds that sample selection bias test and estimation are subject to omitted variables and recommends the study of banks' lending policies to better incorporate the decision-making process in fair lending analysis.

The Heckman's sample selection model is used to conduct empirical studies for two national banks to show the potential impact of underwriting on pricing disparities. Monte Carlo simulations are conducted to illustrate the model estimators' large sample properties and investigate the impact of omitted variables on testing and estimating sample selection bias.

I. Introduction

The fair lending risk assessment of mortgage pricing decisions determines whether similarly situated minority and nonminority borrowers receive differential treatment from mortgage lenders with regard to pricing loans.

The pricing decisions in mortgage lending have become increasingly sophisticated and complex. New loan products with various terms and features are continuously being invented. Note rates are tiered according to borrowers' creditworthiness and loan characteristics. Pricing structures have more flexible fees and points are customized to applicants' capabilities and needs. As a result, mortgage prices are continuous rather than discrete, varying for different borrowers.

This continuation has enabled loan-level statistical analysis and modeling to measure pricing disparities in mortgage lending; for example, see Courchane and Nickerson (1997), Crawford and Rosenblatt (1999), Nothaft and Perry (2002), Black, Boehm, and DeGennaro (2003), Avery, Canner, and Cook (2005); Boehm, Thistle, and Schlottmann (2006), Boehm and Schlottmann (2007), Courchane (2007), Bocian, Ernst and Li (2008). The most commonly used measurements of pricing are the Home Mortgage Disclosure Act (HMDA) rate spread, overage/underage, annual percentage rate (APR), and note rate. In most cases, a single equation approach with an emphasis on supply-side variables was used to measure pricing differences of originated loans. The single equation approach uses ordinary least square (OLS) regression, usually controlled for such factors as borrower creditworthiness, loan characteristics, geographic differences, and market conditions. The demographic dummy is introduced to capture the residual pricing differences attributable to prohibited demographic characteristics (race, ethnicity, and gender) that cannot be explained by other factors. The single equation approach is easy to implement; however, it might be subject to sample selection bias.

As Heckman (1976, 1979) summarized, sample selection bias is basically an issue of nonrandom selection into subsampling, which in practice can be caused by self-selection or data sampling. In the context of fair lending analysis of mortgage pricing, sample selection bias is the result of two factors: (1) simultaneity bias and (2) truncation or partial observability. Simultaneity bias arises when the single equation approach disassociates the pricing decision from other mortgage lending decisions (such as the borrower's choice of loan programs or terms, or the lender's underwriting decision), if these decisions are related to the pricing decision. Partial observability refers to quoting and reporting only the pricing information from originated loans rather than from all applications. Partial observability is less of a problem if the underwriting and pricing decisions are not related, because the originations will be a random sample of all the loan applications and, therefore, the OLS estimator of pricing conditional on its being observed is unbiased. However, partial observability plus the simultaneity bias could complicate matters.

Consider a simplified and hypothesized case like this: both the mortgage underwriting and pricing decisions are based on one single factor—borrower's Fair Isaac Corporation (FICO) score, which is drawn from the same data-generating process and randomly assigned to either the nonminority or the minority group. Two different cases are then simulated. The first case assumes there is no differential underwriting treatment between the two groups but the minorities have to pay a higher rate given the FICO. Under the second case, the minorities have to have a higher FICO than the nonminorities to get approved, and receive a higher rate even if their FICO scores are the same. Under case one, the underwriting decisions are independent of the pricing decisions because FICO is not used in the approval or denial decisioning. However under case two, the underwriting and pricing decisions are linked by the common factor FICO. Since the loan approval or denial decision determines the loan origination population, the underwriting result might affect the fair lending assessment of the subsequent pricing decision. Specifically, the minorities have higher FICO scores due to the higher threshold to receive approval, and higher FICO scores lead to lower rate. If the rates that the minorities receive are low enough, they potentially could conceal the effect of the pricing policies unfavorable to the minorities. In Appendix A, we provided details of the data simulation and regression analysis to show that the concealment could indeed happen.

This paper proposes to consider and evaluate the impact of underwriting decisions on pricing decisions for fair lending risk assessment of mortgage loan rates. To the best of the author's knowledge, no previous paper has looked at mortgage underwriting and pricing decisions simultaneously. Using data from two national banks, we analyzed whether sample selection bias exists between underwriting and pricing decisions. A Monte Carlo simulation was used to search for the best estimator for sample selection bias. On the basis of a comparison of the sample selection method estimators with the single equation method estimator in various

4

scenarios, the full information maximum likelihood (FIML) estimator of sample selection model was deemed to be better.

This paper also points out that the test and estimation of sample select bias between underwriting and pricing decisions is subject to omitted variables. Many researchers have pointed out that omitted variable bias affects the reliability of statistical analysis of fair lending risks of mortgage loans. Their primary arguments are that because of difficulties in obtaining comprehensive information or data considered in mortgage lending decisions, statistical modeling might not include all the factors in its analysis. When the omitted variables are correlated with the applicants' prohibitive demographic characteristics, the resulting analysis shows biased fair lending risk measurement. Most of them (Liebowitz and Day 1993, Zandi 1993, Harrison 1998, Day and Liebowitz 1998, Horne 1997, Stengel and Glennon 1999) analyzed the Boston Fed Study data and suggested that the original conclusion might change if more variables were added. Dietrich (2005) conducted a systematic comparison to show that omitted variables have an important impact on both the estimate of the effect of race and the identification of outliers for review. Here we explore the impact of omitted variables under the simultaneous equation system rather than the single equation context. The focus is on how omitted variables affect sample selection bias test and estimation. Through a second Monte Carlo simulation, this paper shows that omitted variables do affect the sample selection bias test and estimation. The empirical study results were then revisited to illustrate the importance of omitted variables for evaluating the underwriting impact on pricing disparity analysis.

The paper is constructed as follows: The Literature Review section begins the discussion with a brief summary of relevant literature to provide background information. The sections on Sample Selection Model Specifications, Estimators, and Their Properties provide details on the sample selection model. Empirical Studies section presents the empirical analyses conducted on Bank A and Bank B. The next section describes the two Monte Carlo simulations, and the final section presents the conclusions.

II. Literature Review

Several papers have emphasized that mortgage lending decisions are related or sequentially dependent; therefore, fair lending analysis of mortgage loans should involve a comprehensive evaluation of the whole lending process. However, until recently, most researchers did not include the pricing decision.

Maddala and Trost (1982) proposed that proper discrimination analysis should be conducted under a system of simultaneous equations of demand and supply on both denied and accepted loan applications. They compared the estimation results of the proposed models with a single equation model for situations in which the interest rate is endogenous and exogenous. Rachlis and Yezer (1993) expanded Maddala and Trost's proposal. They suggested a system of four simultaneous equations for mortgage lending analysis: (1) borrower's application, (2) borrower's selection of mortgage terms, (3) lender's endorsement, and (4) borrower's default. Assuming that the borrowers had already decided to submit a loan application, Yezer, Phillips, and Trost (1994) suggested a simultaneous equation system composed of borrowers' choice of loan terms, lenders' rejection decision, and default by borrowers. Using the proposed structure as the underlying true model, they conducted Monte Carlo experiments to show that single equation estimation of discrimination in accept-reject decision or default decision is biased. Using the Boston Fed Study data (Munnell et al. 1996), Phillips and Yezer (1996) compared the estimation results of the single equation approach with those of the bivariate probit model (Poirier 1980). They showed that discrimination estimation is biased if the lender's rejection decision is decoupled from the borrower's self-selection of loan programs, or if the lender's underwriting decision is decoupled from the borrower's refusal decision. Ross (2000) jointly estimated loan denials with loan performance. Using Boston Fed Study data and Berkovec and colleagues' (1994) Federal Housing Administration (FHA) data on default, Ross found that the estimated difference in loan denial between minorities and whites becomes zero, after controlling for expected default and other factors. However, the study is based on the combination of two data sets—for conventional and FHA loans—with the assumption that their underwriting models are similar.

Ambrose et al. (2004), Bocian, Ernest, and Li (2008), and Courchane (2007) evaluated mortgage loan pricing in relation to borrowers' participation in loan programs or their choice of loan terms.

Although not for the purpose of fair lending analysis, Ambrose et al. (2004) addressed the sample selection bias and the endogeneity issue in mortgage pricing analysis. To evaluate the effect of government-sponsored enterprise (GSE) purchases on primary mortgage market rates, they compared the mortgage yield spread between GSE and non-GSE loans, controlling for credit risk differentials between the two loans. They used the treatment effects model (Greene 2003) to estimate the conforming or nonconforming loan selection simultaneously with the yield spread difference estimation. Ambrose et al. showed that some of the pricing differences between the GSE and non-GSE loans could be explained by the conforming loan selection outcome. They also argued that loan amount and loan-to-value (LTV) ratio have an endogenous relationship. They constructed a simultaneous equation system of LTV and house value, which is used as a proxy for loan amount to account for endogeneity. The LTV predicted by two-stage least squares (2SLS) regression was then used in the OLS estimation of rate spread to adjust for the endogeneity.

Bocian, Ernest, and Li (2008) analyzed subprime loan price differences between similarly situated minority and nonminority borrowers. Because of limited data, they looked at the HMDA rate spread incidence instead of the magnitude of mortgage prices. Their paper focused on the endogeneity issue. For the potential correlation between loan amount and LTV, they constructed two simultaneous equations and used the three-stage least squares (3SLS) predictions of LTV to update the final result. To account for possible endogeneity between loan price and prepayment penalty, loan products (fixed or adjustable-rate mortgages), or loan purposes (purchase or refinance), they segmented the population and conducted an individual analysis for each subpopulation. Their analyses showed that African American and Latino borrowers were more likely to receive higher rate subprime home loans than were non-Latino white borrowers.

Courchane (2007) considered the lender's pricing decision along with the borrower's decision whether to take out a subprime mortgage. She applied an endogenous switching regression model (Maddala and Nelson 1975) to estimate the probability of a borrower's taking out a subprime mortgage and the APR the borrower received conditional on getting either a subprime or prime mortgage. The endogenous switching model is more flexible than the treatment effects model for estimating the price difference between subprime and prime loans. In the treatment effects model, the selection equation outcome determines the value of the choice dummy in the outcome equation; in the endogenous switching regression model, different outcome equations are used depending on the selection equation outcome.

This paper argues that the loan approval or denial decision determines the loan origination population, so that changes in underwriting policies might affect the fair lending assessment of subsequent pricing decisions. We need a model that can simultaneously estimate the binary underwriting decision outcome and the continuous pricing that is partially observable, depending on the underwriting result. Previous models that tackled sample selection bias in fair lending analysis are not appropriate here. The bivariate probit model used by Yezer, Phillips, and Trost (1994) and Phillips and Yezer (1996) is suitable for estimating a binary outcome. The treatment effects model used by Ambrose and colleagues (2005) and the endogenous switching regression model used by Courchane (2007) do not address the truncation issue. To better measure pricing disparities in mortgage lending, this paper introduces the standard Heckman's sample selection model to test and estimate the existence of sample selection bias caused by interaction between the underwriting and pricing decisions.

To stay focused on this purpose, this paper makes the following assumptions and simplifications:

- The borrower's choices of loan programs and products are set to be exogenous.

- Although loan terms—such as LTV or loan amount—could be endogenous owing to, for example, negotiation between lenders and borrowers, they are assumed to be exogenous.

- The borrower's refusal decision (not to accept an approved loan) and default result are not included in the equation system.

- Prices are observed only on approved and originated loans.

III. Sample Selection Model Specifications, Estimators, and Their Properties

Formally proposed by Heckman (1976, 1979), the sample selection model has been widely used in various fields, especially in labor economics to address wage and labor supply issues. Numerous extensions of the model have been made over the years, such as relaxing the normality assumption, modeling qualitative instead of continuous responses, dropping the truncation component, and using a more flexible outcome equation. The treatment effects model and the endogenous switching regression model mentioned earlier can be considered extensions of the sample selection model.

The standard sample selection model is a simultaneous equation system composed of two equations: (1) a selection equation with a binary dependent variable and (2) an outcome equation with a continuous dependent variable that is truncated on the basis of the first equation's binary outcome. The mathematical expression of the sample selection model is

$$z_i^* = w'_i \gamma + u_i \text{ where } z_i = \begin{cases} 1 & if & z_i^* > 0 \\ 0 & if & z_i^* \leq 0 \end{cases} \quad (1)$$

$$y_i = x'_i \beta + v_i \text{ if } z_i = 1, \quad (2)$$

where z is the variable that determines the observation of the outcome y, and z^* is its latent variable. The regressors w and x are assumed to be exogenous; that is, they are independent of the error terms u and v.

It is also assumed that the cross-equation error terms u and v follow a bivariate normal distribution with zero mean, standard deviations of 1 and σ, and a nonzero correlation of ρ, so the subsampling is not random.

$$\begin{pmatrix} u \\ v \end{pmatrix} \sim BN\left(\begin{pmatrix} 0 \\ 0 \end{pmatrix} \begin{pmatrix} 1 & \rho \\ \rho & \sigma^2 \end{pmatrix} \right) \quad (3)$$

If there is no error correlation between the two equations, the simultaneous equation system is reduced to two independent equations, which means pricing and underwriting decisions can be analyzed individually.

The moments of the sample selection model are

$$E[y_i \mid z_i = 1] = x'_i \beta + \sigma \rho \lambda(w'_i \gamma) \qquad (4)$$

$$\mathrm{var}(y_i \mid z_i = 1) = \sigma^2 \left[1 - \rho^2 \left(w'_i \gamma \lambda + \lambda^2\right)\right] <= \sigma^2 \qquad (5)$$

where $\lambda_i = \phi(-w'_i \gamma)/[1 - \Phi(-w'_i \gamma)] = \phi(w'_i \gamma)/\Phi(w'_i \gamma)$ is the inverse Mills ratio (IMR); $\phi(w'_i \gamma)$ is the normal probability density function of $w'_i \gamma$; and $\Phi(w'_i \gamma)$ is the normal cumulative density function of $w'_i \gamma$.

If the error term distribution is accurately captured by equation (3), the log-likelihood function of the sample selection model can be written as

$$l = \sum_{i \in \{z_i = 0\}} \ln\left[1 - \Phi(w_i'\gamma)\right] + \sum_{i \in \{z_i = 1\}} \left\{ \ln \phi\left(\frac{y_i - x_i'\beta}{\sigma}\right) - \ln \sigma + \ln \Phi\left(\frac{w_i'\gamma + \rho \dfrac{y_i - x_i'\beta}{\sigma}}{\sqrt{1 - \rho^2}}\right) \right\}. \qquad (6)$$

Theoretically, the maximum likelihood estimator based on equation (6) is the full information maximum likelihood (FIML) estimator, because it is generated by estimating the two equations simultaneously. Therefore, it has the property of being unbiased and efficient. But despite all the good properties of the FIML estimator, getting the close-end solution of the estimator is complicated, if not impossible, because the log-likelihood function is nonlinear, with a nonzero correlation of ρ. Empirical estimation through iterative estimation and convergence has typically involved intensive use of computing resources, which made the estimation difficult in earlier years.

To overcome the computational difficulties, Heckman (1976, 1979) proposed a two-step estimation process for the sample selection model by introducing an "omitted" variable, the inverse Mills ratio (IMR). In this approach, we first obtain the maximum likelihood estimator of the selection equation by a probit model and calculate the IMR for each observation using the estimated parameters. Then we estimate the outcome equation on the observed population using an OLS model augmented with the IMR. By introducing the IMR, Heckman generates a consistent and computational efficient estimator for the outcome equation. However, because the two equations are not estimated simultaneously, the Heckman estimator is an limited information maximum likelihood (LIML) estimator and is not statistically efficient.

If we ignore the sample selection bias by disassociating the selection and outcome equations and focusing on the latter, we can generate the OLS estimator conditional on pricing being observed. The conditional OLS estimator can be calculated as

$$b = (X'X)^{-1}X'Y, \text{ where } z_i = 1, \quad (7)$$

and the estimation bias of the conditional OLS estimator will be

$$E(b) - \beta = \sigma\rho(X'X)^{-1}X'\lambda. \quad (8)$$

Since σ is always nonzero, the conditional OLS is unbiased under only two scenarios. The estimation bias of the OLS estimator is reduced to 0 when $\rho = 0$, which means there is no error correlation between the selection and outcome equations, or when $(X'X)^{-1}X'\lambda$ is a 0 vector; that is, the regression of the IMR λ on the exogenous vector of the outcome equation X has an R-square value of 0, which is unlikely, as common factors tend to exist in the underwriting and pricing decisions of mortgage loan applications. The sign of OLS estimator bias depends on the sign of ρ and the coefficient of regression of λ on the corresponding element of vector X.

IV.   Empirical Studies

Besides the hypothesized example in Introduction, this paper conducts two empirical studies to show the potential interaction between underwriting and pricing decisions and its impact on fair lending analysis of pricing.

The empirical studies use the HMDA-plus data of two national banks, Bank A and Bank B.[1] HMDA data are the housing loan data that lenders must disclose under the HMDA. HMDA-plus data are the HMDA data augmented with customer and loan information that is commonly used in mortgage underwriting and pricing decisions, such as FICO score, LTV ratio, and debt-to-income (DTI) ratio. With the HMDA-plus data, we can better capture the potential pricing disparities after controlling for legitimate differences.

---

[1] No information that identifies the two banks or their customers is disclosed here.

Empirical Study of Bank A

The first empirical study is based on Bank A's portfolio of first and second lien, conventional, one-to-four-unit, owner-occupied, refinanced loans decided during calendar year 2008. The study focuses on the fair lending risk assessment of pricing decisions between one particular minority group and the corresponding nonminority group.

In 2008, Bank A originated 189 and 2,683 loans and rejected 501 and 2,506 applications for the minority and nonminority borrowers, respectively.[2] The denial rates were 73 percent for the minority group and 48 percent for the nonminority group. Using APR as the pricing measurement, the average rate for the minority originations was 7.19 percent, compared with 6.98 percent for the nonminority originations—a nominal loan rate difference of 21 basis points.

We estimate the pricing disparities by the conditional OLS estimator, and the LIML and FIML estimator of the sample selection model.[3] The LIML estimator is compared with the FIML estimator to show the trade-off between computational efficiency and statistical efficiency.

The exogenous variables used here include demographic indicator, FICO, LTV, DTI, and first lien indicator. The demographic indicator takes a value of 1 if the applicant is from the minority group and 0 if the applicant is from the nonminority group. The other exogenous variables are intended to control for applicants' creditworthiness and loan characteristics. Assuming that the control factors capture all the legitimate differences, a significant nonzero coefficient of the demographic indicator presents statistical evidence of potential disparate treatment. However, all of that information might not be readily available. And for Bank A, data limits meant that the control variables (FICO, LTV, DTI, and lien status) did not represent the entire set of its mortgage lending policy factors.

---

[2] Some loan applications were approved but not accepted; therefore, not originated. We could add another equation to the simultaneous equation system to model an applicant's decision whether to accept or decline the bank's offer. However, to simplify the analysis and convey the main message, we do not do so.

[3] All the estimations are conducted using SAS software. The OLS estimator is estimated by Proc Reg; Heckman's two-step estimator (LIML) is estimated by Proc Logistic (with the link function being probit) and Proc Reg; and the FIML estimator is estimated by Proc Qlim, which is available only in SAS version 9.2. The P-value of LIML is adjusted by the consistent asymptotic variance and covariance matrix.

Table 1 shows the estimation results for Bank A. The FIML estimation reveals an insignificant cross-equation error correlation ρ of -0.1000, and the augmented OLS of LIML estimation has a highly insignificant, close to zero coefficient of 0.0008 for IMR, both indicating that the sample selection bias is statistically insignificant and, therefore, the underwriting and pricing decisions can be evaluated independently. This finding is supported by a comparison of the conditional OLS, LIML, and FIML estimation results. For potential disparate treatment in underwriting measured by the coefficient of the demographic indicator, the FIML result is similar to that of the LIML—both suggest a significant 20 percent denial rate difference between the minorities and the nonminorities, after accounting for FICO, LTV, DTI, and lien status. For the pricing disparity assessment, the LIML and FIML estimators lead to the same conclusion as the OLS estimator conditional on approval: The minority group received an average APR that was 14 basis points higher than that of the nonminority group (The 7-point difference between this number and the original APR difference of 21 basis points can be explained by credit risk differences between the two groups.). Because the same set of exogenous variables (demographic dummy, FICO, LTV, DTI, and first lien indicator) are used for both equations, the R-square of IMR with respect to the outcome equation exogenous variable set X is expected to be close to 1, consistent with the estimated value of 0.9681.

Note that significant statistics for the demographic indicator do not necessarily indicate disparate treatment in mortgage lending decisions. The statistical analysis result could change by introducing more explanatory variables to replicate the policy or by considering other decisions, such as borrower self-selection.

The signs of FICO, LTV, and DTI are intuitive as well. The negative FICO sign in both equations means that the lower the FICO, the more likely the applicant will receive a denial or a higher APR. Positive LTV and DTI indicate that the higher the LTV or DTI, the more likely the applicant will be rejected or pay more for a loan.

Table 1. Estimation Results for Bank A (total observations = 5,879)

Equation	Variable Name*	OLS Conditional		LIML		FIML	
		Estimate	P-Value	Estimate	P-Value**	Estimate	P-Value
Outcome	Intercept	9.3324	<.0001	9.3346	<.0001	9.1154	<.0001
	Demographic indicator	0.1384	0.0032	0.1385	0.0052	0.1328	0.0047
	FICO	-0.3323	<.0001	-0.3329	<.0001	-0.2997	<.0001
	LTV	0.1926	0.0002	0.1938	0.2339	0.1549	0.0089
	DTI	0.1506	0.0621	0.1519	0.4230	0.0869	0.3613
	First lien indicator	-0.1898	<.0001	-0.1896	<.0001	-0.1963	<.0001
Selection	Intercept			5.2543	<.0001	5.2547	<.0001
	Demographic indicator			0.1982	<.0001	0.1982	0.0044
	FICO			-1.1218	<.0001	-1.1226	<.0001
	LTV			1.8301	<.0001	1.8408	<.0001
	DTI			2.3268	<.0001	2.3215	<.0001
	First lien indicator			0.2333	<.0001	0.2314	<.0001
	IMR (λ)			0.0008	0.9941		
	R-square***			0.9681			
	Rho (ρ)					-0.1000	0.2021
	Sigma (σ)					0.6201	<.0001

* FICO, LTV, and DTI were scaled up by 100 in the regression.

** P-value of LIML is adjusted by the consistent asymptotic variance and covariance matrix.

*** The R-square is from the regression of IMR on the exogenous variables of the outcome equation X.

Empirical Study of Bank B

The second empirical study is based on Bank B's first lien, conventional, one-to-four-unit, owner-occupied, home purchase loan portfolio decided in calendar year 2007. The data set includes pricing information for every application, whether denied or approved.[4] This valuable information allowed us to calculate the conditional as well as the unconditional expectations of the pricing, providing a benchmark for a comparison of different analysis methodologies in the empirical study and later in the Monte Carlo simulations.

In 2007, this bank originated 182 and 3,105 loans and rejected 80 and 416 applications for minority and nonminority borrowers, respectively. The denial rate was 31 percent for the

---

[4] Systematic differences might exist between the prices of denials and the prices of approvals. For example, the APRs for denials might be lower than they would have been if they had been approved, because information is lacking on points and fees.

minority group and 12 percent for the nonminority group. The average APR was 7.76 percent for the minority group and 7.37 percent for the nonminority group. The pricing gap declined from 39 basis points to 5 basis points after the underwriting decision—the average APR was 6.75 percent for minority originations and 6.70 percent for nonminority originations. The change of pricing difference before and after origination suggests the existence of pricing and underwriting interaction.

The modeling analysis of Bank B's pricing disparities was similar to that of Bank A. The control variables include the demographic dummy, FICO, LTV, and DTI. The conditional OLS, LIML, and FIML estimation results are generated and compared with those of the unconditional OLS, which can be calculated because we have the APRs for denied applications.

Table 2 shows the estimation results for Bank B. The underwriting and pricing decisions are highly correlated, as indicated by a significant ρ of -0.8454 from the FIML estimation and a significant IMR coefficient of 10.1202 from the LIML estimation. The estimation results of pricing disparities are consistently different: The OLS estimation on the approvals shows that minorities received a favorable price 39 basis points lower than that offered to nonminorities, while the FIML estimates the difference to be 48 basis points. The OLS estimation of pricing difference on all the applications shows a 27 basis point difference. The LIML shows that the APR minorities received is 18 basis points higher, although the difference is not significant. Using the unconditional OLS result as the benchmark, the conditional OLS has the closest estimation of pricing discrimination, the FIML comes next, and the LIML is the worst.

We expected to see a negative ρ from the FIML estimation. For Bank B, the denial rate for the minority group is almost twice as high as that for the nonminority group. The APR difference between the two groups is 39 basis points for applications and 5 basis points for originations. Thus, the denial decision that adversely affects minorities positively affects the origination price they receive. This explains why the coefficient of λ from the LIML is positive. The IMR is a decreasing function of probit $w'\gamma$, as shown in figure 1. Because the minority group has a high nominal denial rate, the probit $w'\gamma$ is higher than for the

Table 2. Estimation Results for Bank B (total observations = 3,783)

Equation	Variable Name*	OLS Unconditional		OLS Conditional		LIML		FIML	
		Estimate	P-Value	Estimate	P-Value	Estimate	P-Value**	Estimate	P-Value
Outcome	Intercept	8.8036	<.0001	8.4517	<.0001	3.3542	0.2293	7.6674	<.0001
	Demographic indicator	-0.2674	<.0001	-0.3858	<.0001	0.1785	0.7941	-0.4820	<.0001
	FICO	-0.4273	<.0001	-0.3601	<.0001	-4.1501	<.0001	-0.2428	<.0001
	LTV	1.2083	<.0001	1.0428	<.0001	13.2416	<.0001	0.9033	<.0001
	DTI	0.4093	<.0001	0.2699	0.0056	12.8684	0.0002	0.0462	0.6581
Selection	Intercept					0.3834	0.2038	-1.4411	0.0008
	Demographic indicator					0.0965	0.2377	-0.1344	0.1585
	FICO					-0.4650	<.0001	-0.2331	<.0001
	LTV					1.4068	<.0001	1.7333	<.0001
	DTI					1.4842	<.0001	1.4036	<.0001
	IMR (λ)					10.1202	<.0001		
	R-square***					0.9986			
	Rho (ρ)							-0.8454	<.0001
	Sigma (σ)							0.6899	<.0001

* FICO, LTV, and DTI were scaled up by 100 in the regression.

** P-value of LIML is adjusted by the consistent asymptotic variance.

*** The R-square is from the regression of IMR on the exogenous variables of the outcome equation X.

nonminority group.[5] Therefore, minorities tend to have a lower λ. At the same time, the denial decision benefits the minority group in terms of pricing—so lower λ is associated with lower pricing.

Because the same set of control variables is used in the analysis of both underwriting and pricing decisions, the estimated R-square 0.9986 is close to 1. The FICO, LTV, and DTI have the same intuitive signs as those in the empirical study of Bank A. Also, FICO, LTV, and DTI are only the basic policy factors for which we have data; they do not exhaust the factors Bank B used in its lending decisions.

Figure 1. Inverse Mills Ratio (Lambda) and Probit (Gammaw)

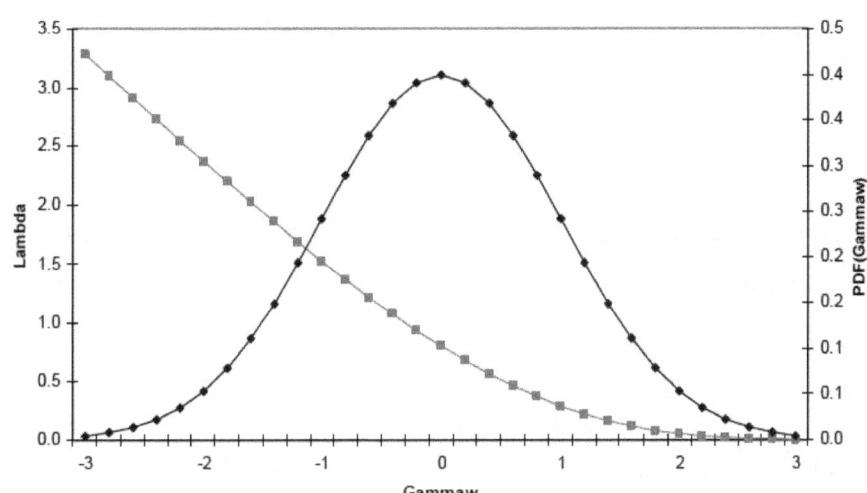

Takeaways from the Empirical Studies

In Bank A, no sample selection bias is detected between pricing and underwriting decisions. In this case, the simple conditional OLS and the sample selection model produce the same result.

Bank B shows high sample selection bias. Theoretically, the sample selection model should be better than the conditional OLS, as it is specifically constructed to address this issue.

---

[5] This does not necessarily imply differential treatment in the underwriting decision. In the case of Bank B, the demographic dummy is not significant in the selection equation by FIML and LIML; therefore, the higher nominal denial rate for minorities is explained by creditworthiness differences.

However, in the empirical study, the conditional OLS result is closer to the unconditional OLS result than to the FIML or LIML. Does this mean that conditional OLS is always better, whether sample selection bias exists or not? Or this is a rare outlier that reflects variation in estimators? To answer that question, we conducted comprehensive Monte Carlo simulations to address the properties of the estimators under various situations.

V.   Monte Carlo Simulations

In Simulation I, we attempt to identify the best method for addressing sample selection bias. In Simulation II, we evaluate the impact of omitted variables on simultaneity bias estimation. Both simulations are based on Bank B's data and were conducted using SAS software.

Simulation I

Data-Generating Process

Under the assumption that they follow a multivariate normal distribution, the moments of FICO, LTV, and DTI are derived from Bank B's data. For the minority group, the empirical parameters are

$$\mu_m = \begin{pmatrix} 653 \\ 94 \\ 46 \end{pmatrix}, \ \rho_m = \begin{pmatrix} 1 & -0.38 & -0.18 \\ -0.38 & 1 & 0.05 \\ -0.18 & 0.05 & 1 \end{pmatrix}, \ \sigma_m^2 = \begin{pmatrix} 5712 & 117 & 132 \end{pmatrix}.$$

For the nonminority group, they are

$$\mu_n = \begin{pmatrix} 734 \\ 78 \\ 41 \end{pmatrix}, \ \rho_n = \begin{pmatrix} 1 & -0.34 & -0.24 \\ -0.34 & 1 & 0.22 \\ -0.24 & 0.22 & 1 \end{pmatrix}, \ \sigma_n^2 = \begin{pmatrix} 3550 & 307 & 151 \end{pmatrix}.$$

The subscript *m* stands for the minority group, and *n* stands for the nonminority group. The exogenous variables are floored and capped by their valid ranges on the basis of actual data, which are [300,850] for FICO, [0,150] for LTV, and [0,100] for DTI.

For the error terms between the selection and outcome equation u and v, bivariate normal distribution parameters are generated on the basis of FIML estimation.

$$\mu = \begin{pmatrix} 0 \\ 0 \end{pmatrix}, \ \rho = \begin{pmatrix} 1 & -0.85 \\ -0.85 & 1 \end{pmatrix}, \ \sigma^2 = \begin{pmatrix} 1 & 0.48 \end{pmatrix}.$$

Because the denial rate difference between the minority and nonminority groups is not significant, the underwriting decision-making process is based on the estimated parameters of the probit model of denial rate with respect to FICO, LTV, and DTI on Bank B applications.

$$z_i^* = 0.4481 + (-0.4761) \times FICO_i + (1.4403) \times LTV_i + (1.4863) \times DTI_i + u_i$$

$$\text{and } z_i = \begin{cases} 1 & \text{if} \quad z_i^* > 0.10 \\ 0 & \text{if} \quad z_i^* \leq 0.10 \end{cases}. \quad (9)$$

The threshold 0.10 is calibrated so that the simulated data have denial rates for the minority and nonminority groups similar to those shown by the true data. For each simulation, 1,000 observations for the minority group and 3,000 observations for the nonminority group are generated. Then the underwriting outcome is assigned, depending on whether the latent variable z_i^* is above the 0.10 threshold or not. The loan application is denied if $z_i^* > 0.10$ and approved if $z_i^* \leq 0.10$. The denial rate is roughly 14 percent for the overall population—about 25 percent for minorities and 10 percent for nonminorities.

APRs are generated for all 4,000 observations using the fitted outcome equation by unconditional OLS on all the applications, including both approvals and denials:

$$y_i = 8.8036 + (-0.2674) \times I_{d_i} + (-0.4273) \times FICO_i + (1.2083) \times LTV_i + (0.4093) \times DTI_i + v_i$$

$$(10)$$

where I_d is the demographic dummy.

Table 3 lists the summary statistics of one simulated data series. The simulated APR takes values from 4.11 percent to 9.73 percent for nonminority borrowers and from 4.68 percent to 10.00 percent for minority borrowers, leading to respective average APRs of 6.78 percent and 7.07 percent The denial rate is 9.80 percent for nonminorities and 25.20 percent for minorities.

Table 3. Descriptive Statistics of a Simulated Data Series

I_d	# Observations	Variable Name	Mean	Std Dev	Minimum	Maximum
0	3,000	Denied	9.80%	0.2974	0%	100%
		APR	6.78%	0.7872	4.11%	9.73%
1	1,000	Denied	25.20%	0.4344	0%	100%
		APR	7.07%	0.8157	4.68%	10.00%

Simulation Design

As shown in equation (8), the performance of the conditional OLS estimator is subject to the endogenous correlation by the cross-equation error terms ρ and the exogenous correlation between X (the exogenous variable set of the outcome equation) and W (the exogenous variable set of the selection equation), represented by an R-square of λ over X. Therefore, the Monte Carlo simulation is conducted for different value combinations of ρ and X. Specifically, ρ takes a value of -0.4, -1, 0, and 0.6 (in addition to the estimated value of -0.85 from the true data). For each ρ, by dropping variables in X that overlap with those in W, data series are simulated in four scenarios to cover various exogenous correlations[6].

Under scenario 1, the outcome equation is generated by equation (10), and X consists of the demographic dummy I_d, FICO, LTV, and DTI. Since W consists of FICO, LTV, and DTI, which is a subset of X, the R-square of λ over X is close to 1.

Scenario 2 drops DTI from X, so the APR generation is

$$y_i = 8.8036 + (-0.2674) \times I_{d_i} + (-0.4273) \times FICO_i + (1.2083) \times LTV_i + v_i, \quad (11)$$

and the R-square decreases to 0.93.

Scenario 3 drops both LTV and DTI from X, and the APR generation equation becomes

$$y_i = 8.8036 + (-0.2674) \times I_{d_i} + (-0.4273) \times FICO_i + v_i. \quad (12)$$

Regression of λ over X leads to an R-square of 0.71.

---

[6] There are nine scenarios if all the variable combinations are considered, here we pick four to representative.

Scenario 4 includes only the demographic dummy to generate the APR.

$$y_i = 8.8036 + (-0.2674) \times I_{d_i} + v_i \quad (13)$$

The R-square is 0.21. The R-square is not zero even if there is no common variable between X and W. That is because the FICO, LTV, and DTI have different distributions for the minority group and the nonminority group, as the data-generating process indicates. This shows why it is hard to find exogenous variables that are orthogonal to the demographic dummy.

Combining different values of ρ and R-square leads to 20 different scenarios. For each scenario, the data simulation and model estimation are repeated 500 times.

Results

The Monte Carlo simulation results are summarized in table 4, with one row for each scenario. The conditional OLS, LIML, and FIML estimations of the demographic dummy coefficient are shown in the columns. For each scenario, the mean and variance of the 500 estimations and (based on those two) the T-statistics ($[mean - (-0.2674)]/ sqrt(var)$) and mean square error (MSE, $[mean - (-0.2674)]^2 + var$), are provided.[7] It is assumed that correct model specification is available for estimation, so the same set of exogenous variables is used for data generation and pricing disparity estimation.

The main findings of Simulation I are as follows:

When there is no endogenous correlation ($\rho = 0$), all the estimators are unbiased and the corresponding variance and MSE are similar. The OLS, being the simplest estimator, has the minimum variance and MSE in three of the four scenarios. That is expected, as OLS imposes the constraint $\rho = 0$ while the sample selection estimators estimate ρ.

When there are endogenous and exogenous correlations, the conditional OLS is biased. The direction of the OLS bias depends on the sign of ρ and the estimated coefficient of I_d in the regression of λ over X. Since λ tends to be lower for minorities, the demographic dummy I_d is expected to have a negative coefficient in the regression of λ over X. Therefore, when $\rho < 0$,.

---

[7] The value -0.2674 is the true coefficient of the demographic dummy.

Table 4. Monte Carlo Simulation 1 Results (*W* includes FICO, LTV, DTI)

X: Simulation and Estimation	R-square	Rho	OLS Conditional				LIML				FIML			
			Mean	Variance	T-Stat***	MSE*	Mean	Variance	T-Stat	MSE	Mean	Variance	T-Stat	MSE
I_d FICO LTV DTI**	1	-0.85	-0.2514	0.7877	0.57	1.0437	-0.2651	0.8060	0.08	0.8111	-0.2667	0.7451	0.03	0.7456
I_d FICO LTV	0.93	-0.85	-0.2495	0.8326	0.62	1.1523	-0.2496	0.8289	0.62	1.1472	-0.2673	0.7976	0.00	0.7976
I_d FICO	0.71	-0.85	-0.2269	0.7331	1.50	2.3774	-0.2496	0.7451	0.65	1.0616	-0.2685	0.6964	-0.04	0.6976
I_d	0.21	-0.85	-0.1425	0.6295	4.98	16.2220	-0.2449	0.7740	0.81	1.2793	-0.2653	0.6282	0.08	0.6327
I_d FICO LTV DTI	1	-0.4	-0.2621	0.9950	0.17	1.0233	-0.2683	1.0197	-0.03	1.0204	-0.2679	1.0077	-0.02	1.0079
I_d FICO LTV	0.93	-0.4	-0.2596	1.0294	0.24	1.0898	-0.2597	1.0285	0.24	1.0886	-0.2672	1.0402	0.01	1.0402
I_d FICO	0.71	-0.4	-0.2485	1.0044	0.60	1.3627	-0.2587	1.0302	0.27	1.1062	-0.2669	1.0289	0.02	1.0292
I_d	0.21	-0.4	-0.2083	0.7738	2.12	4.2630	-0.2557	1.0151	0.37	1.1518	-0.2657	1.0174	0.05	1.0204
I_d FICO LTV DTI	1	-1	-0.2488	0.6762	0.72	1.0225	-0.2654	0.6845	0.08	0.6887	-0.2670	0.0302	0.07	0.0304
I_d FICO LTV	0.93	-1	-0.2472	0.7499	0.74	1.1572	-0.2473	0.7445	0.74	1.1473	-0.2673	0.0340	0.02	0.0340
I_d FICO	0.71	-1	-0.2178	0.6538	1.94	3.1120	-0.2441	0.6871	0.89	1.2281	-0.2676	0.0297	-0.04	0.0297
I_d	0.21	-1	-0.1228	0.5565	6.13	21.4656	-0.2426	0.6552	0.97	1.2713	-0.2671	0.0327	0.05	0.0328
I_d FICO LTV DTI	1	0	-0.2665	1.1480	0.03	1.1489	-0.2667	1.2108	0.02	1.2112	-0.2664	1.1905	0.03	1.1916
I_d FICO LTV	0.93	0	-0.2671	1.1069	0.01	1.1070	-0.2671	1.1049	0.01	1.1050	-0.2672	1.1200	0.01	1.1201
I_d FICO	0.71	0	-0.2683	1.0184	-0.03	1.0192	-0.2680	1.0322	-0.02	1.0325	-0.2677	1.0827	-0.01	1.0828
I_d	0.21	0	-0.2672	0.7810	0.01	0.7811	-0.2666	1.0402	0.03	1.0409	-0.2665	1.0890	0.03	1.0898
I_d FICO LTV DTI	1	0.6	-0.2764	0.9735	-0.29	1.0552	-0.2665	0.9883	0.03	0.9892	-0.2660	0.9697	0.05	0.9716
I_d FICO LTV	0.93	0.6	-0.2781	1.0442	-0.33	1.1576	-0.2780	1.0456	-0.33	1.1580	-0.2660	1.0475	0.04	1.0494
I_d FICO	0.71	0.6	-0.2945	0.8775	-0.91	1.6108	-0.2785	0.9437	-0.36	1.0665	-0.2654	0.9030	0.07	0.9068
I_d	0.21	0.6	-0.3544	0.6927	-3.30	8.2582	-0.2834	0.9451	-0.52	1.2011	-0.2681	0.8321	-0.03	0.8326

* MSE is scaled up by 1,000.

** True coefficient of I_d is -0.2674.

***T-Stat whose absolute value is equal or greater than 1.64 are underlined, which corresponds to 10% significance level under normal distribution assumption.

the conditional OLS is biased upward; when $\rho > 0$, it is biased downward. The Monte Carlo simulation results support this conclusion.

As more exogenous variables are dropped from the outcome equation and there is less and less overlap between X and W, the bias of the conditional OLS increases, because the absolute coefficient of I_d gets larger as the related creditworthiness factors drop. The same pattern is observed from the LIML estimation, although it is not significant. Note that the higher the ρ, the smaller the variance for all the estimators. This is consistent with equation (5).

Overall, the FIML estimator is the winner by MSE except when $\rho = 0$ (the OLS has a slightly higher MSE than the FIML). For measuring pricing disparities, we can start with FIML to test whether $\rho = 0$ or not. If the hypothesis $\rho = 0$ is rejected, FIML is suggested to estimate the pricing disparities simultaneously with underwriting disparities; if the hypothesis $\rho = 0$ is accepted, the single equation approach is recommended because of its effectiveness and simplicity.

Simulation II

In the context of simultaneous equations, we conducted Simulation II to show that the sample selection bias test is subject to the choice of exogenous variables; specifically, that omitted exogenous variables could cause false negatives.

The data-generating process of Simulation II is similar to that of Simulation I. The empirical parameters of FICO, LTV, and DTI are exactly the same. The denial rates are simulated using equation (9), and the APRs are simulated using equation (10). The only difference is that ρ is set at 0, so there is actually no sample selection bias in the simulated data.

However, in contrast to Simulation I, Simulation II allows for omitted variables in the estimation of the outcome equation. We tested nine scenarios in which the X variables were different combinations of I_d, FICO, LTV, and DTI. The results are shown in table 5. The first scenario shows that without omitted variables, the sample selection bias test correctly shows the underlying model. Scenarios 2 through 8 are cases with omitted common variables; scenario 9 is a case of an omitted noncommon variable, as I_d is unique to the outcome equation. As the T-statistics show, the null hypothesis of $\rho = 0$ is rejected if common exogenous variables are omitted, even though the underlying data are generated with $\rho = 0$. This shows that omitted common variables could lead to a false negative on the sample selection bias test. Under scenario 9, although dropping the noncommon exogenous variable I_d does not reject the null hypothesis, the T-statistics rises to 1.41.[8]

Table 5. Monte Carlo Simulation II Results

W	X		FIML Estimation of Rho		
Simulation/Estimation	Simulation	Estimation	Mean	Variance	T-Stat
FICO LTV DTI	I_d FICO LTV DTI	I_d FICO LTV DTI	-0.0076	0.0587	-0.03
FICO LTV DTI	I_d FICO LTV DTI	I_d FICO LTV	-0.3584	0.0133	-3.11
FICO LTV DTI	I_d FICO LTV DTI	I_d FICO DTI	-0.6670	0.0017	-16.17
FICO LTV DTI	I_d FICO LTV DTI	I_d LTV DTI	-0.7503	0.0008	-25.98
FICO LTV DTI	I_d FICO LTV DTI	I_d FICO	-0.6957	0.0012	-20.44
FICO LTV DTI	I_d FICO LTV DTI	I_d LTV	-0.7706	0.0008	-26.58
FICO LTV DTI	I_d FICO LTV DTI	I_d DTI	-0.8347	0.0004	-43.21
FICO LTV DTI	I_d FICO LTV DTI	I_d	-0.8494	0.0002	-55.10
FICO LTV DTI	I_d FICO LTV DTI	FICO LTV DTI	0.2236	0.0253	1.41

Theoretically, we can rewrite equation (4) as

$$E[y_i \mid z_i = 1] = x'_i \beta + \sigma\rho\lambda(w'_i \gamma) = x'_{1i} \beta_1 + x'_{2i} \beta_2 + \sigma\rho\lambda(w'_i \gamma) = x'_{2i} \beta_2 + \left(\frac{x'_{1i} \beta_1}{\sigma\lambda}\right)\sigma\lambda, \quad (14)$$

where x_{1i} are the omitted exogenous variables and x_{2i} are the nonomitted exogenous variables of the outcome equation. Given $\rho = 0$ the term $\sigma\rho\lambda(w'_i \gamma)$ equals 0. And the outcome expectation can be rewritten as $x'_{2i} \beta_2 + \left(\frac{x'_{1i} \beta_1}{\sigma\lambda}\right)\sigma\lambda$ if x_{1i} are omitted in estimating outcome equation. Then the sample selection bias test becomes a test of whether $\frac{x'_{1i} \beta}{\sigma\lambda} = 0$ instead of $\rho = 0$. If x_{1i} are the omitted variables that are common to the outcome equation's exogenous variable vector X and the selection equation's exogenous variable vector W, x_{1i} and λ are related, $\frac{x'_{1i} \beta}{\sigma\lambda}$ is non-zero. If x_{1i} are non-common omitted variables orthogonal

---

[8] However, this does not downplay the importance of capturing the noncommon factors for the analysis.

to λ, then the sample selection test is not affected. But usually even if x_{1i} are noncommon omitted variables, they are not totally orthogonal to λ; and when their correlation is high enough, non-common omitted variables could also lead to the false negative of the sample selection bias test.

We then revisited the empirical study of Bank B. The initial analysis shows a highly significant cross-equation error correlation of -0.8454 with FICO, LTV, and DTI as the control factors. We were able to collect the documentation-type information that is an important factor in Bank B's mortgage lending decisions. The inclusion of this information as an additional variable drastically lowered the error correlation, from -0.8454 to -0.2915, and the magnitude of corresponding T-statistics decreases from 29.17 to 2.47 with a negative sign.

The finding from Simulation II reinforces the importance of replicating the decision-making process while conducting statistical analysis. The statistical analysis should be based on a good understanding of the institution's polices and processes.

VI. Conclusion

Mortgage lending is a comprehensive and complicated process. It involves the choice of programs and product terms—a selection process that might be based on the borrower's assessment of information and assistance provided, or the result of bargaining and negotiation between borrower and lender. Lenders' decisions are likely to be affected by expectations about borrowers' performance. The mortgage application outcome involves multiple factors, such as approved or not, percentage rate, fees, and how fast the loan can be closed.

This paper suggests evaluating potential disparities in mortgage pricing by taking other loan decisions into consideration. Specifically, it evaluates the potential sample selection bias between the mortgage underwriting and pricing decisions. Using Heckman's standard sample selection model, the empirical studies show statistical evidence of sample selection bias, suggesting an interaction between underwriting results and pricing differences among minority and nonminority borrowers.

The paper also investigates the impact of omitted variables on testing and estimating sample selection bias. A Monte Carlo simulation proves that omitted variables could lead to or add to the simultaneity bias. To address this issue in fair lending analysis, the paper emphasizes the importance of studying banks' lending policies to determine best practices in the decision-making process.

References

Ambrose, B., M. LaCour-Little, A. Sanders, and P. Calem. 2004. The Effect of Conforming Loan Status on Mortgage Yield Spreads: A Loan Level Analysis. *Real Estate Economics*, 32(4), 541–569.

Avery, R., G. Canner, and R. Cook. 2005. New Information Reported under HMDA and Its Application in Fair Lending Enforcement. *Federal Reserve Bulletin*, 91, 344–394.

Berkovec, J., G. Canner, S. Gabriel, and T. Hannan. 1994. Race, Redlining, and Residential Mortgage Loan Performance. *The Journal of Real Estate Finance and Economics*, 9, 263–294.

Black, H., T. Boehm, and R. DeGennaro. 2003, Is There Discrimination in Mortgage Pricing? The Case of Overages. *Journal of Banking and Finance*, 27, 1139–1165.

Bocian, D., K. Ernst, and W. Li. 2008. Race, Ethnicity and Subprime Home Loan Pricing. *Journal of Economics and Business*, 60, 110–124.

Boehm, T., and A. Schlottmann. 2007. Mortgage Pricing Differentials across Hispanic, African-American, and White Households: Evidence from the American Housing Survey. *Cityscape: A Journal of Policy Development and Research*, 9, 93-136.

Boehm, T., P. Thistle, and A. Schlottmann. 2006. Rates and Race: An Analysis of Racial Disparities in Mortgage Rates. *Housing Policy Debate*, 17, 109–49.

Courchane, M. 2007. The Pricing of Home Mortgage Loans to Minority Borrowers: How Much of the APR Differential Can We Explain? *Journal of Real Estate Research*, 29, 399.

Courchane, M., and D. Nickerson. 1997. Discrimination Resulting from Overage Practices. *Journal of Financial Services Research*, 11, 133–151.

Crawford, G., and E. Rosenblatt. 1999. Differences in the Cost of Mortgage Credit Implications for Discrimination. *The Journal of Real Estate Finance and Economics*, 19, 147–159.

Day, T., and S. Liebowitz. 1998. Mortgage Lending to Minorities: Where's the Bias? *Economic Inquiry*, 36, 3–28.

Dietrich, J. 2005. Under-Specified Models and Detection of Discrimination: A Case Study of Mortgage Lending. *The Journal of Real Estate Finance and Economics*, 31, 83–105.

Greene, W. 2003. *Econometric Analysis*. Upper Saddle River, NJ: Prentice Hall.

Harrison, G. 1998. Mortgage Lending in Boston: A Reconsideration of the Evidence. *Economic Inquiry*, 36, 29–38.

Heckman, J. 1976. The Common Structure of Statistical Models of Truncation, Sample Selection and Limited Dependent Variables and a Simple Estimator for Such Models. *Annals of Economic and social Measurement*, 5, 475–492.

Heckman, J. 1979. Sample Selection Bias as a Specification Error. *Econometrica: Journal of the Econometric Society*, 47, 153–161.

Horne, D. 1997. Mortgage Lending, Race, and Model Specification. *Journal of Financial Services Research*, 11, 43–68.

Liebowitz, S., and T. Day. 1993. A Study That Deserves No Credit. *Wall Street Journal*, 1, 14.

Maddala, G., and F. Nelson. 1975. Switching Regression Models with Exogenous and Endogenous Switching. *Proceedings of the American Statistical Association*, 423–426.

Maddala, G., and R. Trost. 1982. On Measuring Discrimination in Loan Markets. *Housing Finance Review*, 1, 245–268.

Munnell, A., G. Tootell, L. Browne, and J. McEneaney. 1996. Mortgage Lending in Boston: Interpreting HMDA Data. *American Economic Review*, 86, 25–53.

Nothaft, F., and V. Perry. 2002. Do Mortgage Rates Vary by Neighborhood? Implications for Loan Pricing and Redlining. *Journal of Housing Economics*, 11, 244–265.

Phillips, R., and A. Yezer. 1996. Self-Selection and Tests for Bias and Risk in Mortgage Lending: Can You Price the Mortgage If You Don't Know the Process? *Journal of Real Estate Research*, 11, 87–102.

Poirier, D. 1980. Partial Observability in Bivariate Probit Models. *Journal of Econometrics*, 12, 209–217.

Rachlis, M., and A. Yezer. 1993. Serious Flaws in Statistical Tests for Discrimination in Mortgage Markets. *Journal of Housing Research*, 4, 315–336.

Ross, S. 2000. Mortgage Lending, Sample Selection, and Default. *Real Estate Economics*, 28, 581–621.

Stengel, M., and D. Glennon. 1999. Evaluating Statistical Models of Mortgage Lending Discrimination: A Bank-Specific Analysis. *Real Estate Economics*, 27, 299–302.

Yezer, A., R. Phillips, and R. Trost. 1994. Bias in Estimates of Discrimination and Default in Mortgage Lending: The Effects of Simultaneity and Self-Selection. *Journal of Real Estate Finance and Economics*, 9, 197–215.

Zandi, M. 1993. Boston Fed's Bias Study Was Deeply Flawed. *American Banker*, 19, 13.

Appendix A. Effect of Underwriting on Fair lending Pricing Analysis

We simulated 1,000 FICO scores from a random normal distribution with a mean value of 720 and a standard deviation of 60. Then the FICO scores were randomly assigned to the nonminority and minority groups evenly. The nondifferential underwriting policies approve any applicants with a FICO above 700; but the differential underwriting policies approve nonminority applicants whose FICO is above 650 but only approve minority applicants with a FICO above 800. The mortgage rate is determined by the equation $(14 - 0.01*FICO + 0.2*demo\_ind)$ plus a random error term following a standard normal distribution. The demo_ind equals 1 if the applicant is from the minority group, and equals 0 otherwise. So the pricing policies state that the mortgage rate goes down by 1 percent if FICO goes up by 100 points; and the minorities will be charged 20 basis points more given other things equal. The statistics of the simulated data series are listed in table A1. Since the FICO scores are generated by the same random process, they are fairly similar for the nonminorities and minorities. The variable approval1 is the approval rate under case one. It is about the same for the two groups because the underwriting policies are the same for situation one. The rate1 is 21 basis points higher for minorities on average, which is consistent with the rate generating process. Under case two, the approval rate approval2 is much higher (86 percent compared with 8 percent) for nonminorties since the underwriting policies favor the nonminorities. The minorities appear to have lower mortgage rate (5.93 percent compared with 6.69 percent) on average.

Table A1. Statistics of Simulated Data

Demo_ind	Variable	N	Mean	Std Dev	Minimum	Maximum
0	fico	500	716.36	59.76	505.60	889.31
	rate1	303	6.45	1.06	3.07	9.21
	approval1	500	61%	0.49	0%	100%
	rate2	432	6.69	1.09	3.07	9.73
	approval2	500	86%	0.34	0%	100%
1	fico	500	719.80	61.89	487.39	933.64
	rate1	319	6.65	1.12	3.47	10.32
	approval1	500	64%	0.48	0%	100%
	rate2	39	5.93	0.84	3.47	7.67
	approval2	500	8%	0.27	0%	100%

Next we conducted fair lending analysis of mortgage pricing to see if we can capture the disparate treatment in the pricing policies. The method we used is the common single equation approach. For case one, we were able to capture the pricing decisioning factors accurately: the coefficients of FICO and the demo_ind are significant and consistent with the underlying data generating process. However for case two, the regression analysis could not detect the differential treatment as structured in the pricing policies as show by the insignificant coefficient of variable demo_ind. Table A2 provides the details of the regression results.

Table A2. Regression Result

Case 1			
Variable	Intercept	FICO	Demo_ind
Coefficient	13.06	-0.01	0.22
T-statistics	16.41	-8.34	2.64
Case 2			
Variable	Intercept	FICO	Demo_ind
Coefficient	13.29	-0.01	0.17
T-statistics	19.60	-9.76	0.88

We argue that the reason single equation approach could not detect the pricing disparities here is that it does not account for the interaction between the underwriting and pricing decisions. As figure A1 illustrates, when underwriting policies do not differentiate between the two groups, the single regression on originations can accurately capture the FICO and demo_ind effect at the pricing stage. And as figure A2 shows, when underwriting policies favor nonminorities, the minority population is skewed with higher FICO at the pricing stage, which conceals the effect of the pricing policies unfavorable to the minorities.

.

Figure A1. Pricing Analysis with Nondifferential Underwriting Policies

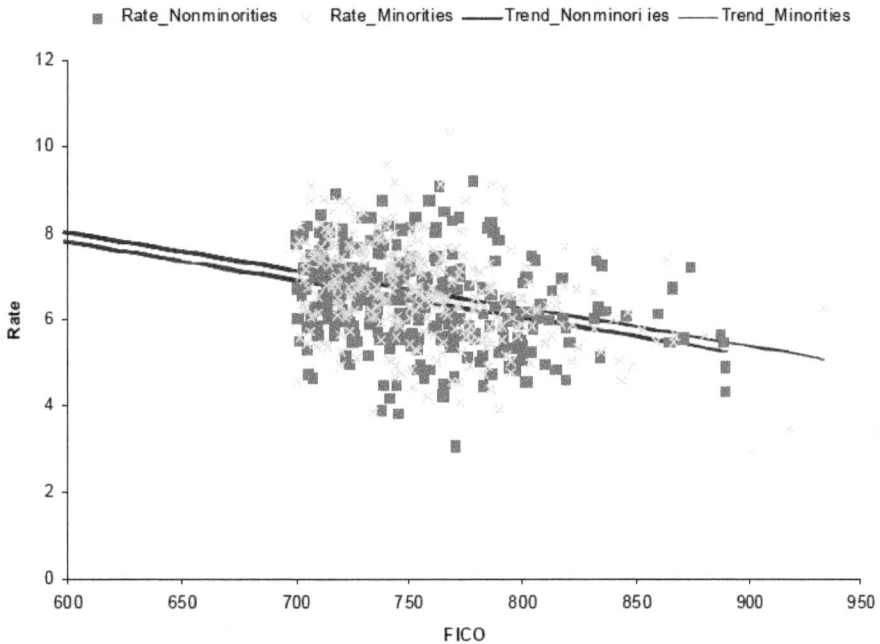

Figure A2. Pricing Analysis with Differential Underwriting Policies

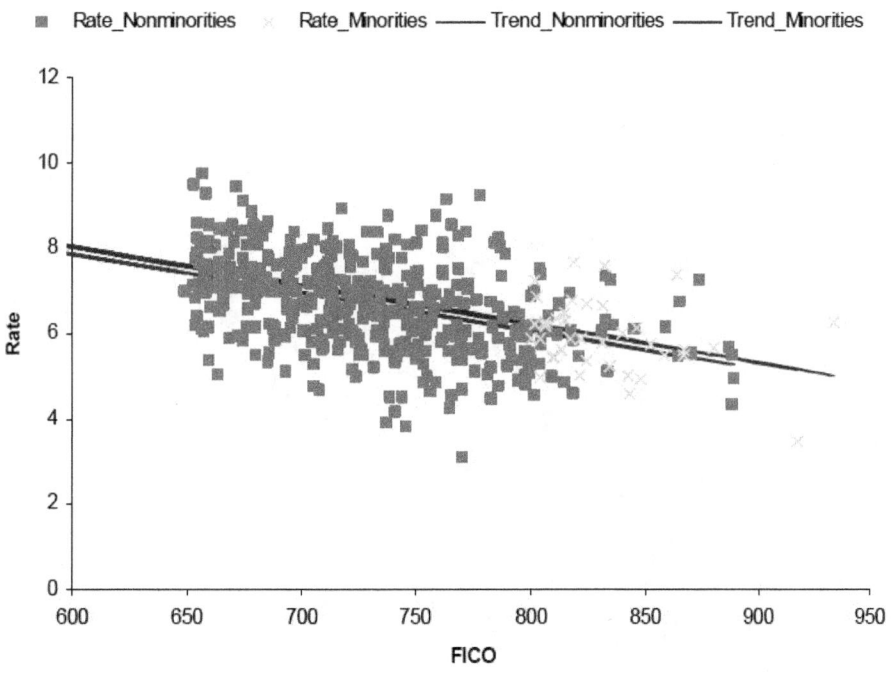

www.ingramcontent.com/pod-product-compliance
Lightning Source LLC
Chambersburg PA
CBHW052026280526
45793CB00005B/1146